CHOOSE YOUR OWN CAREER ADVENTURE

CRUISE SHIP

Monique Vescia

Created and produced by
Bright Futures Press, Cary, North Carolina
www.brightfuturespress.com

Published by
Cherry Lake Publishing, Ann Arbor, Michigan
www.cherrylakepublishing.com

Photo Credits: cover, Shutterstock/Rawpizel.com; page 5, Shutterstock/Rawpizel.com; page 5, Shutterstock/Banana Republic Image; page 5, Shutterstock/DTH; page 7, Shutterstock/Andrey Armyagov; page 8, Shutterstock/Antoniu; page 9, Shutterstock/Alzay; page 9, Shutterstock/Alexey V Smirnov; page 11, Shutterstock/Voloh; page 13, Shutterstock/Oleksandr Kalinichenko; page 13, Shutterstock/Baramee Thaweesombat; page 15, Shutterstock/Everett Historical; page 17, Shutterstock/gbaustista87; page 17, Shutterstock/Lightspring; page 19, Shutterstock/chrishumphreys; page 21, Shutterstock/Maksin Rumiantcev; page 21, Shutterstock/Iakov Filimonov; page 23, Shutterstock/donvictorio; page 25, Shutterstock/ER_09; page 27, Shutterstock/Robert Schlie; page 27, Pavel L Photo and Video; page 29, Shutterstock/karenchm; page 29, Shutterstock/ILYA AKINSHIN; page 29, Shutterstock/Olga Gavrilova.

Library of Congress Cataloging-in-Publication Date

CIP has been filed and is available at catalog.loc.gov.

Printed in the United States of America.

CHOOSE YOUR OWN CAREER ADVENTURE

CRUISE SHIP

Prepare to Set Sail!

Get ready to **embark** on a high seas adventure! Cruise ships provide ultimate dream vacations for more than 20 million passengers every year. Passengers travel in luxury, as enormous ships transport them from one exotic port to another. While aboard, guests enjoy pools, spas, IMAX theaters, art auctions, and even Broadway plays.

A cruise ship can be as tall as a 25-story skyscraper and as long as four-and-a-half football fields. The best ones are like amazing floating resorts! Some, like Royal Caribbean's *Harmony of the Seas*, carry more than 5,000 passengers at a time. This ship features 16 decks, 20 restaurants, 7 "neighborhoods," and a 10-story spiraling waterslide.

It's not difficult to imagine why cruise ships are cool places to work. Get on deck—it's time to consider which cruise ship positions might be a fit for *your* future career.

All aboard! It's time to choose your own cruise ship adventure!

TABLE OF CONTENTS

CAPTAIN

Experienced ship **captain** needed to embark on a seafaring life aboard luxury cruise liner. Must have excellent **navigational** and leadership skills. Ideal candidate will be licensed graduate of the U.S. Merchant Marine Academy or a state maritime academy. Benefits include excellent salary, lots of prestige, fancy cabin, and extensive travel around the world.

- ***Ready to take on this challenge?***
  Turn to page 6.
- ***Want to explore a career as Chief Purser instead?***
  Go to page 9.
- ***Rather consider other choices?***
  Return to page 4.

Dock your own cruise ship online at **www.freeonlinegames.com/game/easy-cruise**.

Full Speed Ahead

The skies look good for a day at sea. A ship full of passengers is waiting for you to cast off for seven days of fun and sun in the western Caribbean. You'll leave soon from Miami and head for Casta Maya, Mexico. Other **ports of call** include Belize and Honduras. You'll make one last stop in Cozumel before bringing the ship back to port. Passengers are counting on you for smooth sailing all the way. Cruising is a dream vacation for them.

Come to think of it, this is a dream job for you. Your career at sea started on much smaller vessels. You graduated to larger boats like ferries and freighters, spending many hours at sea. You learned how to handle large vessels in all kinds of weather and can now navigate your way around the world.

At the Helm

Now here you are, **captain** of a megaship! You are responsible for one of the largest cruise ships in the world. You're boss to a couple thousand employees and host to thousands of guests. Ahoy, Captain! Welcome to another week at sea.

You make a final inspection, checking that everything is in tip-top shape. Even a small dent in the ship's **hull** can cost a cruise line nearly $1 million in damages. You are not about to let that happen, not on your watch.

You spent much time practicing on a **simulator** before you ever stepped up to the **helm** of an actual cruise ship to commandeer. The company made certain you had lots of training before your first day on the job.

King of the Ship

From the **bridge,** you have the best view of anyone onboard. You can see **fore** and **aft,** and the endless ocean spreading out ahead. You give the weather one last check, review the maps of the vessel's route, and scan the list of scheduled ports of call. Managers from every crew on the ship radio in to give you the all-ready signal.

As the ship's commander, you are the most important person aboard. Your word is law! In the ship's main dining room, the captain's table is a place of honor. Every passenger hopes to be chosen to sit at your table. You've made some interesting new friends that way.

As you take the wheel of the huge vessel, you vow to give your passengers the trip of a lifetime—and to bring them back safely. Bon voyage!

Your Captain Career Adventure Starts Here!

EXPLORE IT!

Ships all over the world use nautical flags to communicate. Find out which International Code of Signals (sent by flags, lamps, or radio) mean the following:

Man overboard

No, or negative

Yes, or positive

Keep clear

Do not pass ahead of me

TRY IT!

Map Your Route

Pick a region of the world you'd like to visit, and choose five **ports of call** where you want to stop during the voyage. Popular cruise destinations include Alaska, the Caribbean, and Mexico. Some cruise lines travel all the way south to Antarctica and north to Iceland.

The Ultimate Captain's Table

It's a huge honor to be chosen to sit at the captain's table. Choose seven famous people or celebrities to join you as dining companions. What will you talk about to keep the dinner conversation cruising smoothly?

CHIEF PURSER

Cruise line looking for number-cruncher to serve as chief **purser** on luxury ship. Have you been treasurer of every club you've ever belonged to? Do you do Sudoku puzzles for fun and algebraic equations to relax? Solid background in accounting required. Count all the reasons why sailing the seven seas is the right career for you!

- ***Ready to take on this challenge?***
  Turn to page 10.
- ***Want to explore a career as Chief Radio Officer instead?***
  Go to page 13.
- ***Rather consider other choices?***
  Return to page 4.

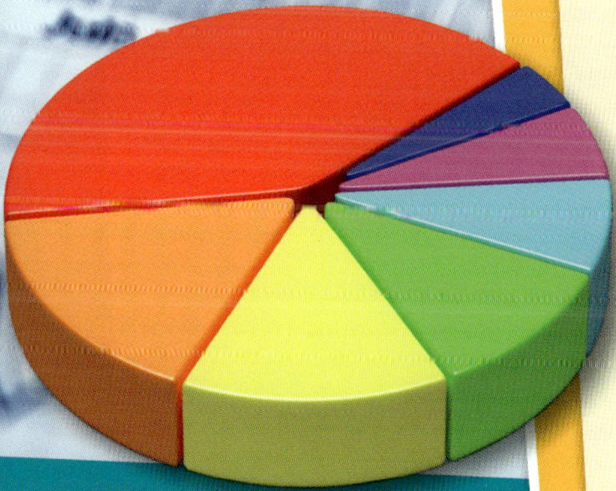

See what it's like to be a chief purser at **http://bit.ly/ChiefPurser**.

Money, Money, Money!

It's Saturday, and have you been busy! You are the ship's **chief purser**. You are called that because you hold the ship's purse strings. You are in charge of all the money on board the cruise ship. Your job started early this morning when you settled the financial accounts of the passengers **disembarking** from the ship.

Then there were the 700 tons of supplies you had to deal with. During the week, your staff ordered all the provisions the ship needed for the next cruise—including thousands of pounds of ice cream and 18,000 rolls of toilet paper. Before setting sail again, you make sure there is enough food on board to lavishly feed thousands of people for a new week. Your staff will process and pay all the **invoices** from **vendors** during the week.

All in a Day's Work

Don't forget that it is payday too! You handle payroll for a couple thousand crew members. They work hard to keep passengers safe, fed, and entertained all week! Fortunately, much of this is done online. You and your accounting team handled the details during the previous week at sea. With one last look at your spreadsheets and ledgers, you press "Send" to deposit paychecks into employees' accounts.

Follow the Money

As chief purser, you are responsible for dealing with millions of dollars every week. You must account for every penny that comes in and every penny that goes out. You are entrusted with the combination to the ship's safe and handling currency from every port of call the ship visits. Passengers come to you with questions and sometimes with complaints. You are the go-to money person, and it is a very big job.

Now, it's time to welcome the new passengers as they **embark** on the ship. You must set up a financial account for each guest. Fortunately, you have help! You have efficient systems in place, and your team is well-trained (by you, of course). In what seems like no time at all, you are ready to set sail again!

Your Chief Purser Career Adventure Starts Here!

EXPLORE IT!

Use your Internet search skills to find out what kind of money is accepted in the following ports of call:

1) *Bali, Indonesia*
2) *Manila, Philippines*
3) *Puntarenas, Costa Rica*
4) *Dubrovnik, Croatia*
5) *Flam, Norway*
6) *Apia, Samoa*
7) *Kusadasi, Turkey*
8) *Durban, South Africa*

(Answers: 1. rupiah, 2. peso, 3. colon, 4. kuna, 5. krone, 6. tala, 7. lira, 8. rand)

TRY IT!

Add It Up!

Your luxury cruise ship can carry 4,000 passengers. If everyone shells out $1,600 for a week-long cruise, how much does the cruise line earn before operating expenses? Use your calculator to figure it out. Extra credit: What's the total if half of that sum pays the workers' salaries?

How Do They Do It?

Cruising is a very profitable business, so how does the company make so much money? Food and entertainment are free. But other attractions cost guests extra. There are spas, casinos, gift shops, and more. Make a list of all the different things passengers can buy aboard ships. Cha-ching!

CHIEF RADIO OFFICER

Top radio officer needed to do the talking for new cruise ship. Experienced graduate of maritime school and familiar with high-tech shipboard communication systems preferred. Must be fluent in **Morse code, NATO phonetic code**, and **maritime** flag language. Ability to stay calm in a crisis a plus. Full-time travel aboard the world's most luxurious cruise ships required.

- ***Ready to take on this challenge?***
  Turn to page 14.
- ***Want to explore a career as Cruise Director instead?***
  Go to page 17.
- ***Rather consider other choices?***
  Return to page 4.

Send an SOS signal at **www.pbs.org/wgbh/amex/rescue/sfeature/sos.html**.

Hello, World!

Cruise ships spend days and even weeks at sea—far from dry land and civilization. Your job as the ship's chief radio officer is to stay in touch with the rest of the world. This includes keeping in touch with the home office and others on shore, and communicating with other ships you encounter at sea.

You report to the main deck department where the captain and other officers also work. Stepping into your work area is like entering into a high-tech wonderland. There are switchboard systems, satellite phones, and telegraph machines for keeping ship-to-shore communication open and available for crew and guests. During your shift, you make phone calls, send telegrams, and keep in contact with all nearby ships.

Storm Tracker

Monitoring the weather is one of your most important responsibilities, and there is plenty of cool equipment to help you do that job. Conditions can change very quickly at sea, so you and your staff provide regular weather updates to the captain. The last thing you want to do is be caught unaware by a hurricane!

Every radio message sent to and from the ship is recorded in a logbook. Luckily, you speak three languages, and this skill comes in handy more than you might expect. You work in four-hour shifts so you can stay alert and vigilant. Part of your job as chief is to schedule other officers and assistants to rotate between on- and off-duty status each day.

Save Our Ship

Nearly everyone knows the sad story of the *Titanic*. The only firsthand, real-time record of what happened that freezing night in April 1912 is the collection of radio messages sent out from the sinking ship. The luxury cruise liner's "wireless" operators sent distress signals to all nearby vessels, saying, "Hurry to the rescue!" Without the radio operator's distress signals from the *Titanic*, there would likely have been no survivors.

When necessary, you use special emergency signals to alert other members of the crew without alarming the passengers. If a passenger falls off the ship, "Mr. MOB," or three long blasts of the ship's whistle, means Man Overboard! "Bravo, Bravo, Bravo" means there is a fire or other serious incident on board. Some cruise lines have their own codes.

Thankfully, no distress signals are necessary today!

Your Chief Radio Officer Career Adventure Starts Here!

EXPLORE IT!

Radio operators use code words to make sure their messages are clearly understood. Look up the NATO phonetic alphabet and figure out how to spell:

Your name

SOS

The port you'd most like to visit from a cruise ship

TRY IT!

Learn Morse Code

In the past, radio officers had to know Morse code, a communication system that uses a series of dots and dashes by sound or light to transmit words and numbers. Search online for the Morse code alphabet. Once you've mastered it, you and your friends can use flashlights to send secret messages to one another!

Weather Log or Knot?

In February 2016, the cruise ship *Anthem of the Seas* ran into a severe storm off the Carolina coast and had to return to port after the vessel was damaged. Weather conditions at sea can change quickly. For a week, check the day's weather report in the paper or online and notice how accurate the forecast is. Record your data in a weather log.

CRUISE DIRECTOR

Looking for someone to be the life of the party on board one of the world's most amazing cruise ships. This job is all about fun, entertainment, and keeping thousands of passengers happy while sailing from one exotic port of call to another. Theatrical experience a plus. Anyone looking for a typical 9-to-5 job need not apply.

- ***Ready to take on this challenge?***
  Turn to page 18.
- ***Want to explore a career as a Ship Engineer instead?***
  Go to page 21.
- ***Rather consider other choices?***
  Return to page 4.

Find a cruise theme that floats your boat at **http://themecruisefinder.com**.

Good Morning, Cruisers!

Passengers start their days with fresh air, coffee, and *you*. As the **cruise director**, your morning broadcasts are eagerly awaited as guests plan another fun-filled day. Options vary depending on whether the ship is sailing or docked at a port of call. You cheerfully announce the day's activities and encourage passengers to get out there and have a blast!

You are the ship's party girl or guy! You organize and host onboard social activities and entertainment events. Your workplace is a huge resort that floats in the ocean. Today's megaships are enormous, and it's your responsibility to keep thousands of passengers busy and entertained during each week-long cruise. From full musical productions to costume contests to gourmet cooking classes, there's always something exciting going on! You've got to be on top of it all.

Don't Worry, Be Happy

You are the public face of the cruise company, always smiling and eager to answer passengers' questions. When passengers come aboard the ship, you are right there—front and center—to welcome them. Your crisp white uniform is the first of many outfits you will wear today. Once all the guests are aboard, you hustle downstairs to your **cabin** to change. You are scheduled to judge a diving contest in the afternoon, so you choose a bright Hawaiian shirt, linen pants, and a floppy straw hat. Don't forget your megaphone and clipboard! In the evening, you'll need clothing that is more formal to host a magic show.

Life of the Party

You've always been social and outgoing, and you love chatting up the ship's passengers. They are always happy to see you, whether you're welcoming them into the dining room or calling out moves for a line dance. They erupt in applause when you grab a microphone and sing along as the band plays one of your favorite songs.

Your job is fast-paced and exciting. What's not to like about encouraging people to be happy all day?

Your Cruise Director Career Adventure Starts Here!

EXPLORE IT!

Visit the website of several cruise lines to find out what types of activities they advertise for the following guests:

Children *Teens*

Adults *Senior citizens*

TRY IT!

What Would You Wear?

A cruise director needs a big wardrobe for a busy day. What clothes would you wear for the following activities?

Greeting passengers as they board the ship

Emceeing a disco dance contest

Hosting a formal dinner

Giving a talk about scuba diving excursions

Create an Event Schedule

Plan a day's worth of fun on the ship. Start in the morning, and pack the day with exciting events until bedtime. Be sure to include activities that cruisers of all ages will enjoy. Think about special excursions they can do while in port. Beaches, shopping, sightseeing ... Snorkeling, anyone?

SHIP ENGINEER

Mechanically-minded engineer needed to take charge of machines and keep massive cruise ship running without embarrassing or dangerous glitches. Must know the difference between an engine, boiler, and motor. Ideal candidate is handy with tools and endlessly curious about how stuff works. Perks include free room-and-board and travel to places most people only dream about visiting.

- ***Ready to take on this challenge?***
  Turn to page 22.
- ***Want to explore a career as a Steward instead?***
  Go to page 25.
- ***Rather consider other choices?***
  Return to page 4.

Find out how a ship propeller works at **www.explainthatstuff.com/how-propellers-work.html.**

Keep It Moving!

You are a **ship engineer**—make that the *chief* cruise ship engineer. The four yellow stripes on your shoulder, called **epaulettes**, signify your rank. Your crew members call you "sir" or "ma'am." Your main job is to keep this floating playground going.

An engine is a machine that converts energy into motion. It takes a lot of force to move a vessel the size of a cruise ship through the water. A megaship's engine has the power of 50,000 horses. Because these engines are enormous and extremely heavy, the engine room must be located at the lowest part of the ship to keep it stable.

The engine area, where you work, takes up three whole decks of the ship. The space is divided into smaller compartments for safety reasons. In the event a problem occurs in one compartment, the damage can be contained.

Lead the Way

You lead a crew of highly skilled workers. Your team makes sure that the ship's main engines work properly and you regularly inspect their work. Sometimes you even climb down inside the huge engines to check for wear and tear. Of course, you only do this when the engines are not running!

Today, everything looks good. You double-check the emergency generators and electrical systems, test the heating and cooling systems, and run checks on ventilation and plumbing. All systems are go! Just what you like to see.

In the Guts of the Ship

Down in the belly of the ship, spaces can be tight and ceilings are low. It's also very noisy down there when the ship is in motion. You and the other engineers have to raise your voices to be heard. Over time you've learned to tell the difference between the normal sounds the ship's engine makes and those that signify trouble. The sound of engines humming along without problems is like music to your ears.

Many of today's ships use gas turbines. These engines are more energy efficient than the earlier diesel engines, but they still use a lot of fuel. Propellers, called screws, provide forward and reverse motion.

Even so, your huge ship moves rather slowly through the water. The average speed of a cruise ship is 20 knots, or about 23 miles (37 kilometers) per hour—even when the captain orders "Full steam ahead!"

Your Ship Engineer Career Adventure Starts Here!

EXPLORE IT!

Go online to find out what function each of these machines plays on-board a cruise ship:

Boiler

Engine

Propeller

Ventilator

Wastewater treatment system

TRY IT!

Sink or Float?

How does a metal ship stay afloat? Take the Foil Boat Engineering Challenge: You'll need a square sheet of foil and four drinking straws. Use these materials to build a boat no larger than 6 x 6 x 6 inches (15.2 x 15.2 x 15.2 centimeters). Your boat must float and not tip over easily. See how many pennies you can add, one by one, before your foil boat sinks.

How Do Engines Work?

Before you know how to fix an engine, you have to know how it works. Investigate how engines work, and use what you discover to make a diagram or model showing how engines make things go.

STEWARD

Neat freak needed to provide top-notch customer service to passengers aboard luxury cruise ship. Duties include housekeeping and hospitality as you care for passengers' every need. Ability to work quickly, efficiently, and cheerfully a must. Off time spent enjoying onboard staff amenities and exploring the world's most desirable vacation spots.

- ***Ready to take on this challenge?***
  Turn to page 26.
- ***Want to explore a career as a Captain instead?***
  Go to page 5.
- ***Rather consider other choices?***
  Return to page 4.

Learn how to make all kinds of towel animals at **www.maketowelanimals.com.**

May I Help You?

It's up and at 'em for your job as cabin **steward**. Your day on the ship starts first thing in the morning. With your assigned guests either at breakfast or off on excursions, you hustle around freshening their cabins. You pick up stacks of freshly washed towels and sheets from the ship's laundry area and stock a cart with everything else you need: miniature bottles of shampoo and body wash, shower caps, and cleaning supplies.

Towel folding is an art form on cruise ships, and it is one of your favorite parts of the job. It's your chance to get creative and connect with the guests. You know how to fold a towel into an elephant, a monkey, or a turtle wearing sunglasses!

Cabin Comforts

You put new soaps and other personal grooming products (called "toiletries") in the guests' bathrooms and make their beds. There's vacuuming and dusting to do too. You leave a card with your name on it, so guests know who to call if they need anything. Pampering passengers is what you do best!

Later in the day, you come back to turn down the bedsheet and refill the mini-bars in every cabin. You also leave copies of the daily schedule, so the guests know the events for the next day. A chocolate placed on each pillow adds a nice good-night surprise.

Squeaky Clean

Cleanliness is very important on a cruise because illness can spread quickly in the contained environment of a ship. Norovirus, better known as the stomach flu, spreads from person to person. You have heard of nasty outbreaks of flu on other ships. It does not sound like fun for passengers or crew! Many passengers get terribly ill, and there are unpleasant messes to clean up. You don't want this happening on your ship. That's why you take extra care to clean all surfaces and leave clean drinking glasses in every room. You frequently wash your hands too, with hot water and soap.

Your hard work pays off at the end of each cruise. That's when passengers show their gratitude by leaving you monetary tips or presents. It's so nice to be appreciated!

Your Steward Career Adventure Starts Here!

EXPLORE IT!

Ship stewards encounter people from many different nationalities every week. Go online to find out how to say "hello," "thank you," and "good-bye" in the following languages (and then practice what you learn):

French

Portuguese

Japanese

Italian

Spanish

TRY IT!

Start a Mini Collection

If your family takes a trip and stays in a hotel, you can start a collection of teeny-tiny toiletries. Most motels and hotels offer these free to their guests. Ask your friends to bring you back some samples when they travel. See how many different kinds you can collect.

Make Your Cabin Shipshape!

In the tight spaces of a cruise ship, everything needs to be stowed tidily away. Start with your own room. Make sure your bed is neatly made and all your stuff is tucked away where it belongs. Your parents will be astonished and you will enjoy your ship-shape space!

WRITE YOUR OWN CAREER ADVENTURE

WRITE YOUR OWN CAREER ADVENTURE

You just read about six awesome Cruise Ship careers:

- Captain
- Chief purser
- Chief radio officer
- Cruise director
- Ship engineer
- Steward

Which one is your favorite? Pick one, and imagine what it might be like to do that job. Then write your own career adventure!

Go online to download free activity sheets at www.cherrylakepublishing.com/activities.

ATTENTION, ADVENTURERS!

Please do NOT write in this book if it is not yours. Use a separate piece of paper.

GLOSSARY

bridge
forward part of the ship, from where it is steered

cabin
passenger room on a ship

captain
person in charge of a ship

chief purser
person in charge of all the money onboard a cruise ship

cruise director
person who organizes and hosts the social activities and entertainment events on a ship

disembarking
exiting the ship, usually at the end of a cruise

embark
to get on a ship that is ready to travel

epaulettes
ornamental shoulder straps that signify rank

fore and aft
front to back of a ship

helm
a tiller or wheel and any associated equipment for steering a ship or boat

hull
outer shell of a ship

invoices
detailed bills for goods shipped to a customer or for work done or to be done for a customer

maritime
having to do with the sea, ships, or navigation

Morse code
alphabet or code in which letters are represented by combinations of long and short signals of light or sound

NATO phonetic code
The 26 code words in the NATO phonetic alphabet are assigned to the 26 letters of the English alphabet in alphabetical order as follows: Alfa, Bravo, Charlie, Delta, Echo, Foxtrot, Golf, Hotel, India, Juliett, Kilo, Lima, Mike, November, Oscar, Papa, Quebec, Romeo, Sierra, Tango, Uniform, Victor, Whiskey, X-ray, Yankee, Zulu

nautical
having to do with ships and sailing

navigational
the act or practice of navigating, or planning or directing the course of a vessel

ports of call
destinations where ships stop during voyages

radio officer
person in charge of ship-to-shore communications

ship engineer
person who takes care of the cruise ship's engines

simulator
machine featuring a set of controls like those found in an actual ship used to train captains in their navigation skills

steward
someone who serves passengers on a ship

vendors
people who sell things

INDEX

ABOUT THE AUTHOR

Monique Vescia worked in children's book publishing before embarking on her own career as a writer. She is the author of 25 nonfiction books on a variety of subjects, ranging from A (animal behavior) to Z (author Markus Zusak) and nearly everything in between. She lives in Seattle, Washington, with her husband and teenage son, and she keeps bees in her backyard.